Written by
J. J. PATRONE

IZZY B.
MAKES A
PIZZA

Illustrated by
EMILY ASHMORE

Illustrated by Emily Ashmore.

Archway Publishing books may be ordered through booksellers or by contacting:

Archway Publishing
1663 Liberty Drive
Bloomington, IN 47403
www.archwaypublishing.com
1 (888) 242-5904

ISBN: 978-1-4808-7222-6 (sc)
ISBN: 978-1-4808-7221-9 (e)

Print information available on the last page.

Archway Publishing Rev. date: 3/22/2019

ARCHWAY
PUBLISHING

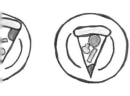

FOR MY sweetest Izzy B, who delights me each day in her quest to learn and grow.

Hello pizza shop!
It's time to make the pizza.

There's lots to do
before we start,
Let's pre-heat the oven,
that's the first part.

Put on your apron
and here we go,
Let's turn on the mixer
to make the dough.

we make the sauce
Right on time,
blending tomatoes
fresh off the vine.

Always cook
with a
GROWN-UP

we gather our veggies
and meats alike,
we're getting good now,
it's like riding a bike.

We stretch the dough
evenly across,
Go ahead, pick it up
and give it a toss!

We add our cheese
about a half a pound,
making sure to spread
it evenly around.

The oven is hot so
Let's get Ready,
slide the pizza in
nice and steady.

Our pizza is cooked
just golden brown.
Let's take it out and
put it down.

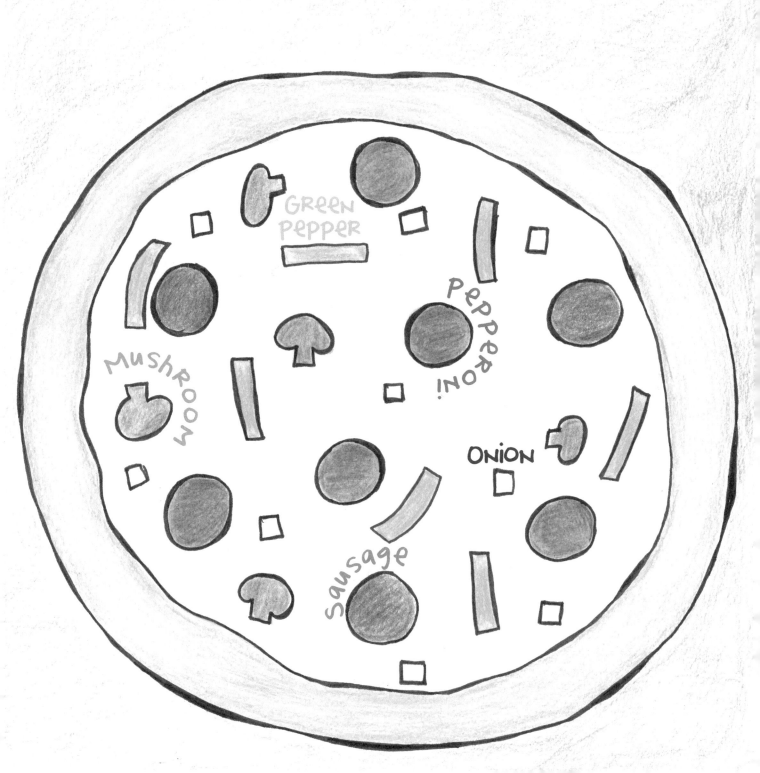

We grab our cutter
and slice it into eight,
our friends are hungry
and can hardly wait.

We serve the pizza
to smiling faces,
our friends are here from
all different places.

We say a blessing to God above,
who has provided this pizza
out of His love.

We thank you for this food we eat
this wonderful pizza with
veggies and meat.

It's fun to work and serve others
because God made us all
sisters and brothers.

"Thanks for having fun and making pizza with me" -Izzy B-

About the Author

J. J. Patrone is the owner of a pizzeria in Holden Beach, North Carolina, an actor in the film 8 Slices, a member of the US Coast Guard Reserves, a husband, and a father of three great kids. He has learned a lot from life, mostly that God should be at the center, and fun should be all around.

Printed in the United States
By Bookmasters